Knocked Out without Being Punched

DINAH M. SULLIVAN

ISBN 979-8-88751-324-9 (paperback)
ISBN 979-8-88832-316-8 (hardcover)
ISBN 979-8-88751-325-6 (digital)

Christian Faith Publishing
832 Park Avenue
Meadville, PA 16335
www.christianfaithpublishing.com

Printed in the United States of America

To the heartbeat of my son, Braxton D. Washington Sr.

His memory will forever be with me: his strength, courage, love for others, and the laying down of his life to save others. He was strong, courageous, charismatic, loved by most, but hated by some others—others that wanted to be like him.

He poured out all he had to the people in his circle, helping and encouraging them in every way. I was captivated by knowing that he was teaching and preaching to his friends a week before his untimely demise (*everything took place with him*). All his friends remembered him asking them one question, the one question that they could not answer: what's the one thing man can't escape? They did not know the answer, but he told them, "Death."

Death was the only thing he never feared because he said, "You have to stay ready for it." His friends and family were angry with him because that was all he was talking about the week before death took place, as if he were preparing them to get ready for it.

Thank you for the embodiment of being true to who you were. His life may have been taken away violently, but no one can take away a memory.

Though he slay me, yet will I trust Him.

—Job 13:15 (KJV)

Contents

Acknowledgments

I would like to pour out my gratitude to my family and friends for their support, tenacity, and persistence in standing with me while I endured heartache, pain, and weakness.

A special thank-you to a man so precious, even when I thought he turned his back on me in my weakest moment. I realized he is yet a special part of me, my husband/Kieran, for standing in the face of adversity and not walking away from me during my fiery trial. Also, for his persistence in helping me to put pen to paper and the time he took sifting through the pages of my broken heart and encouraging me to complete the process. Thank you.

Mighty grateful for my armor-bearers: Minister Mary L. Favors of Forerunner to the Nations ministry/FTTN; my brother Thomas Washington for coming to the rescue of my husband, and his wife, Carol Washington, who dedicated her arms to me faithfully; Brian Atherton, my manager, for getting me all the assistance I needed and being a lifeline for my family; Peggy Ladd, who walked with me through the trenches of heartache and stayed the course; my spiritual mom Mae Jackson for the words of encouragement.

I thank my loyal friends: Diane Tharpe, for coming to my rescue at work; Margaret Harris; and Shawna Christian, for feeding the mass of people.

Thank you to the Wiggins family, the Nelson family, Ministers Marvin Easley, Barry Briscoe Ray, Bishop Drayton, and countless other friends and family.

Thank you to all my children: Bobby, Sade, Brandon, Kevin, Kiara, and Little Braxton, for seeing about me.

Also, my special friends Brenda and Gary Bible helped me push through and make this happen so others can hopefully be blessed. I thank especially Brenda, for allowing her husband to take time from her to dedicate to me for this process.

A special thank-you to all the people that helped carry me along the way.

Please! Forgive me if I overlooked anyone. Much love to you all!

As I Think of You

One morning, the sun opened its eyes to the grandeur of another day, and there you were, a little boy, a breathing and moving bundle of joy gracing the world with your presence. And like the sun begins to rise and warm the earth, you begin to grow and warm the hearts of the people around you.

There were days when clouds rolled in and blocked the sun, and you felt gray, not feeling your best. Some days, you would hide behind the fog of the day. Then the atmosphere would change, and so would you, piercing from behind the fog as good as new.

Always taking time to talk with people for a while and drawing them in with your loving and kind ways. The elders around you were in awe of your confidence, and your name alone, they said, carried with it strength. How you ministered downtown to those in need and how you'd give the clothes off your back or the shoes off your feet or your last penny, if it would help someone.

There were some dark days for you and some skies of gray, growing and learning, but you didn't always obey. You can't learn on this journey unless you make a few mistakes and have some heartaches and setbacks, but onward, you would tread until you bounce back.

Just like I am in awe of the vistas from the sun shining through the trees, I am thankful just knowing your spirit was so free, free to be kind and free to love. That could have only come from above.

You came into the world and did what you were supposed to do with the time God had given to you.

Your time was short-lived, and the sun began to go down and slowly close its eyes with the darkness of the night's sky. Although, there will never be another sunrise because it has been set for you.

Your existence and the story of your life still warms my heart just thinking of you. You were like the morning dew waiting to greet anyone you encountered. The blanket of the morning dew that covers the ground, and every time I see it, I feel like God is covering me with his resounding love, and his love has no bounds.

Yes, I yearn to see your face and hear your voice again. I miss you telling me, "I love you, and don't let people get to you like that, it's not that serious."

I still feel the emptiness inside without you being here. When everyone comes around, and you are not here, I always imagine you being somewhere close by.

I thought you would be the one to lead the family after I was gone off the scene.

Your brothers, sisters, friends, and family miss you terribly. They feel no one loved them as you did, and you paved the way for them with the older generation. They lost their brother and their best friend.

You were like a shepherd over sheep. When the shepherd is away, the sheep scatter. And did they scatter. You were the best brother ever.

You lived your life to the fullest, just like the sun that rose and warmed hearts and gradually set so we could see the light of the shining moon.

You warmed many hearts and faded away too soon. But I thank God for every day I had with you. I think of you often, especially when the sun is shining.

Even in the night's light of the shining moon, I envision your smiling face so filled with grace as I envision you looking back at me.

The only sadness I have is knowing that your children will never get to know or feel all the love you had to share. But your spirit lives on because we keep your memory alive for them.

At least I get to enjoy your three children. What a joy it brings to my soul because I see reflections of you through your children. Always loved.

Introduction

I've had the pages of this book written in my heart for many years now. And one morning, I decided to get up and write about everything I was feeling and the thoughts that were raging inside of me.

I didn't want whatever I was going to write to be something massive. I just wanted it to be relative to the point of helping myself heal inwardly.

Writing this book has been cathartic, a way for me to release the hurt and pain I felt that flooded my soul. During this writing process, I hoped that maybe it could help someone else facing a similar situation. Since my spirit was flooded with emotions, I decided to write what I was feeling the best way I remembered it.

I felt like a dam that was overflowing, and I had to find a way to release the pressure.

Writing about my pain has given me solace. For a while, *I felt like God must really hate me*. Why else would he allow this to happen to me if my love for him was so strong?

I was torn apart so much so that it felt like the largest vacuum in the world had sucked all the life out of me. I felt like I had been knocked out so cold that I would never be able to get up, a weakness where people had to hold me up for me to stand. When they weren't holding me up, I was crying and screaming out of control in exasperation until I would fall back into a comatose state of being.

I didn't have the breath to answer a phone call, just the thought of hearing, "*I'm sorry for your loss*," intensified my pain.

After a few years of intense suffering, I remembered being out in my garage where we used to have church on Sundays. This particular day, I was grieving over my son, and for some reason, I picked up the first Bible I saw and opened it. I began to read the page it opened up to, and from that page, this verse captured my attention:

> *Your eyes saw my unformed body; all the days ordained for me were written in your book before one of them came to be.* (Psalm 139:16 NIV)

It's amazing how you can read something over and over but never get the message until it's time for you to receive the message. Lo and behold, I got the greatest lesson of my life, and there it was, God gave me an answer to my heart's cry.

I said, "Okay, God!"

That day was going to happen before he was born. That passage of scripture gave me peace, and I decided to get up and try to live. *I realized God "did not" hate me.*

Today, I am at peace.

> *God does give beauty for ashes.* (Isaiah 61:3 KJV)

When Everything in Your World Seems to Be Going Great, Watch Out

There are times when we get caught up in life, allowing nothing to faze us. We go about life doing the mundane things people typically do from day to day. We succumb to the weight of daily tasks. We began to put off things and people. You know, the things we used to do, such as check in on a friend or call someone out of the blue just because you were thinking about them to make sure things are going well with them. We get so busy that we don't have time to do the minuscule things, and we keep telling ourselves, "*We'll call them tomorrow.*"

But "tomorrow" keeps being *tomorrow, next week,* or *next month.* And we keep putting it off, and before we know it, this so-called *tomorrow* has turned into years!

I was so caught up in doing me and having a marvelous relationship with the Lord. I felt like I was on top of the world, and nothing could touch me. I had a mountaintop experience. I truly felt like no weapon formed against me would prosper.

I was basking in the glory of life, having a typical day one day and the next day being awakened to an overwhelming joy in my spirit. I was elated with happiness. It was a peculiar happiness, one I'd never felt before. Everywhere I went and everything I did or said, I laughed, cracked jokes, and made people smile and their day a little brighter.

This happiness came from an unusual place, a place I knew not of, nor could I explain. Happiness exuded from every pore of my body.

Then about midweek, I begin to think to myself, *This must be it, I must be getting ready to die!* Because I was always told, on your best day, you are sick enough to die. I began to believe my days were nearing or coming to an end.

I called my sister and told her how I had awakened to this overwhelming happiness, and maybe I was getting ready to die. She said, "No, sometimes things like that happen."

At the end of my being overwhelmed by joy and happiness, I didn't know I was about to be *knocked out without being punched*.

I got a call asking me if I had seen or heard from my son that Thursday morning. I said, "No, I hadn't seen or heard from him, why?" They said they had heard on the news that shots were fired at the apartment complex where my son was, and no one had heard from him, nor could they get an answer on his phone. We were all thinking maybe he went over to visit one of his friends.

I got nervous and panicky and said he would show up or call if something was wrong. For some strange reason, I kept waiting for him to show up. In my mind, I kept seeing him jump over the fence in the backyard like he was running for his life. I didn't know what was going on, but I felt troubled in my spirit.

I went to bed, and before waking up Friday morning, I had a dream. In the dream was a lot of commotion, but we were in a church setting, and everybody was at church waiting for him to show up because he was supposed to be the speaker for that day.

But he never showed up.

I woke up in the dream but was not awake yet. I saw myself talking to a friend of mine in the dream, and I remember telling her, *"It's not fair, your son shot someone, and he gets to live, but my son died."*

When I woke up, I went into prayer but felt so uneasy and on edge. I had to get ready to get the bus to go to work for the day, and I told my spouse that I wasn't coming home after work because I hadn't heard from my son, and it was not like him not to give me a call or come by my house and tell me what was going on at his house.

I left home and got the bus to go to work, but just before getting off the bus, one of the girls that worked in the same building came from the back of the bus as we were getting ready to get off at our stop and asked me, "How are your children?"

There arose a stammer, a stutter on my tongue, and my mouth began to say, "*Dead?*" Dead? I put my hand over my mouth because I knew not where those words came from, but it seemed like the pit of my soul was crying out before I ever even knew what had happened.

We got off the bus and walked the rest of the way to the job, and my heart began to get heavy, but I knew I had to go to work. A while later, I had to deposit a letter into the mailbox down the street, so on my break, I went to mail the letter, and as I was walking, my heart got heavier with each step.

As I turned to go back to the building, my heart got intensely heavy with a spirit of death, and I remember saying, *"Lord, I know I am getting ready to die, but please let me make it back to the building where someone knows me and can call my family when I fall dead."*

As soon as I entered the building, I felt like I was going to drop dead right then and there. But I didn't. I made it to my desk, and my phone rang as soon as I got to my desk. It was my daughter.

She said, "Mama, we found him." And she paused, so my heart was elated, ecstatic, and overjoyed for a brief moment!

Then she said, "He's dead."

I couldn't say a word. I hung up the phone and went to my manager and told him, "I got to go. Someone has killed my son."

He jumped up and escorted me out of the office and called for a taxi to take me wherever I needed to go. I had the taxi take me home, but no one was there, so I called my spiritual mother to come to pick me up, and she came right away. We began to drive to the place where my son was or the scene, and she began to tell me, "Don't get out here and act like God is not in control, you will need to contain yourself and stay calm when we get there."

I had no response to her words, but for some reason, when she picked me up, I sat in the back seat of her car.

When we arrived at the scene, all I could smell was death. I laid down on the back seat of the car, and while there, the sting of death hit me very hard.

I couldn't contain myself, and I began to scream so loud that it seemed like it came from the end strands of my hair all the way down to my toenails. I felt stripped to the very core of my being, and I was kicking and screaming until someone came and got me out of the car. I ran up to see if that was really my son, but the police stopped me.

Someone was with me (I don't remember who), but I began to run down the street. I'd lost sight of myself, but I do remember my oldest son ran and stopped me and held on to me with a tight grip.

I remember sitting in someone else's car with my spiritual mom, and I felt uneasy being in there and had to get out.

Then my husband, sister, and brother showed up, and I don't know where my oldest son was, but I was left standing with my husband, sister, and brother. I lost sight of my children and everyone else around me.

All that joy and happiness I felt prior to this escaped me. Now I'm left with unknown feelings and not knowing what to do. I was asking myself, "Who would want to murder my child?" He was loved by everybody. He wouldn't harm a soul. His entire life was about making people laugh and smile and helping anyone he came into contact with; he had no enemies. *"How did this happen to my son?"*

We stayed on the scene until midnight. I tried to see him before they loaded him into the coroner's van, but they still would not let us see him. That didn't make sense to me.

My spiritual mother had left earlier, and everyone else was gone, and my husband and I, with my sister and brother, were the only ones left at the scene of the crime. As the coroner drove off with the police behind them, we left as well.

The People Closest to You Will Speak Harsh Words at an Inopportune Time

As we were driving home, my husband turned to me and said the worst thing ever. He said, "I hope you aren't planning to have a funeral, just dig a hole, throw him in it, and bury him."

Those words stung me with intensifying anger toward my husband, so much so that I had to turn my head away from him.

We got home, my sister and brother came over, and we all sat around the table, but something had taken over my husband. It was like a blanket of anger that came over him; he got a baseball bat and began walking through the house, ranting and raving with words that I'd never heard coming out of his mouth.

He was overcome with this stirring emotion of anger, and I mistook his anger as being toward me; when in reality, he was just angry because of what happened to my son.

In my agony, I felt like he had turned against me. Nothing positive came out of his mouth to me, and he wouldn't embrace me or the reverse. The negative words that came from his lips only made me draw back further from him. I felt like he was coming against me when I needed him the most. I began not to want his love or embrace, and I even stopped talking to him. In the midst of all that, I knew our grandson was with us, but I'd lost sight of him. I didn't remember him being anywhere near me. I lost sight of myself and everyone around me; I was in a total state of shock.

We were all in the dark—baffled because no one had told us anything. Not the police, not the people that lived in that house, nothing. We were clueless.

Amidst all that, I remember telling my sister that I needed her help with this while my brother looked after my husband.

While he had succumbed to anger, I'd succumbed to fear and anger. I became so angry with my husband that I didn't even want to see him.

Because the next day, his anger intensified to the point where he didn't want the rest of my children to come over; he wanted to change all the locks on the doors of the house and wanted to change the phones.

I realized he was just as scared as I was, but I never gave any thought to what he might be feeling. Because my children and I were very close, and he was just their step-father.

Disbelief

I was not angry with God, because I had such a relationship with the Lord that I could not believe he would allow this to happen to me. I found myself saying to the Lord, *"Didn't you know he belonged to me?"*

And I heard him reply, *"My son belonged to me, but I gave his life so the world could be saved."*

Shortly thereafter, the news came on, and I heard that a woman had lost all five of her children at the hands of her own husband. I remembered thinking, *I think I'm going through something*, and this woman has lost *all* her children. If I feel the way I do, I can only imagine the hurt she is feeling right now.

Here I am feeling what I feel after losing my child, and I thought there could be no greater pain in the world. But her pain must have been intensified five times greater than anything I was feeling or experiencing.

Feeling Cold and Numb in a Total State of Shock and Confusion

Meanwhile, I felt like the largest vacuum in the world had just sucked all the life out of me. I felt like a hollow shell of a person, and the best way I can describe it is that I felt like an empty wagon that rattles. My bones felt like rattling bones.

I didn't know how I was walking around or standing up because I couldn't eat or sleep. I just remember someone telling me to breathe and drink some water. All I could do was cry myself into oblivion.

My sister became my mouthpiece, eyes, and ears. I became too weak to fight or do much of anything.

At this point, the phone began to ring in the house insanely crazy, and floods of cards began to come in the mail, or people would stop by and bring or drop off a card. As I began to read the cards, I got so irritated that I quit reading because it kept reminding me that my son was gone. It seemed like each card I read was piercing through me.

I Was Filled with Pain and Anger

The cards read as such: "*I'm sorry for your loss,*" or "*With deepest sympathy,*" or "*My condolences to you and your family, you are in our prayers.*"

The calls coming in were the same, so much that I grew angrier, and I couldn't take reading those words anymore. And I was so tired of hearing it on the phone that I just threw the phone as far away from me as I could. They were empty words to me.

Although I know every one of the people that sent the cards meant well and had me and my family's best interests at heart with their warm regards, I had had enough.

I began to reflect back on people that had lost loved ones, and one popped into my mind rather quickly. I remembered telling my daughter's godmother when she lost her son that "*I was so sorry for her loss*" that it brought chills to me, and I was grieved behind the thought of saying that to her.

Because I didn't know what *loss* was until I lost my son. And as I pondered, I cried even more, thinking, *What in the hell does it mean to tell someone you are "sorry for their loss" or "with deepest sympathy" when you don't even know what loss is until you experience it for yourself?*

I can tell you one thing, that is a road no mother or father wants to travel down. It leaves you stricken to the core. To the very essence of your being, it will take you to a place in your mind that you know not of. It's like you left the world and journeyed to an empty place, and no one is there, just you and you alone. You don't know what to say and what to do, and you can't pray.

This place is cold, dark, and scary, and you can't feel anything. No mindset, no real thoughts, and you can't see who is around you or even know that people are there. You can't hear their conversations even though they are talking, no knowledge of places or things. You are like a blank slate, nothing but emptiness inside.

You don't know if you're hurt, have no concept of time, and have no feelings.

Just that something has knocked you so far down you don't know how to get up, overtaken by some force that has taken your mind, body, and soul.

I woke up to shower, but I stood there in agony until the water turned so cold that I couldn't take the coldness of the water anymore. I slid to the floor in the shower in so much agony, trying to wish my child back to life, but I knew that wouldn't happen. It's like someone stripped you of something precious, something you needed and never wanted to get rid of.

A body blow takes the substance out of you.

Preview

Later, we got a call that we could go to the funeral home to see his body. We did, and I saw my son lying there. His mouth was opened enough for me to see his teeth, and it looked like he had a smile on his face. I was waiting for him to say something to me; my heart was glad as if we were going to have a conversation.

I took a closer look and saw a big gaping hole in the front and back of his head, and I couldn't contain myself. From the depths of my soul, I cried! Probably with the loudest cry in the land.

I remember lying on his chest but don't remember how I ended up outside. Someone was with me, and I remember them telling me to breathe.

Once I got outside, I saw the people that were thought to be involved that created the events that led to my son being shot.

They came and stood by me and wanted to hug me, but something in me would not allow me to hug any of them, especially the person he was with when this happened. I remember looking at her, and I believed I heard the spirit of the Lord say to me, *"Look her in the eye* and tell her that *her life will never be the same."*

After that evening, I don't remember much of what else was going on.

> *Dearly beloved, avenge not yourselves, but rather give place unto wrath: for it is written, Vengeance is mine; I will repay,* saith the Lord. (Romans 12:19–21 KJV)

Miss Deceitful Came By

A lot of people began to come by my house as they found out what happened to my son. However, there was one lady that really befriended my husband and began to feed him lies about the incident. I didn't know why he was so angry with me or the rest of my children. But I found out that she told him that my son was murdered by gang members, and they were looking to kill the rest of my family. She stirred up his spirit with her stream of lies. He was afraid and confused.

Basically, I was in the worst place in life that I could be (losing my child), and to add insult to injury, she caused my family more grief.

He believed and held on to her every word against my family.

Somehow, I managed to be in the same area of the house he was in, and I said, *"If you're angry with me and my children because of the information you are getting from her, you need to be aware that I know her very well, and she is a habitual liar. So if she's your source of information, don't believe it."*

By then, it didn't matter to him because she was the only one that was feeding him *any* information. She had drawn him into her clutches. She began visiting him every day, and he was drawn into her clutches and welcomed her presence.

I Was Too Weak to Fight

My grandson is in my care, and I happen to dress him and put him on a red shirt because *I love red! Red* signifies and represents the blood that Jesus shed for me and because my grandson looks good in red!

Two things happened: first, an officer went onto my son's *Facebook* page and saw a picture of my son holding his child, my grandson. Then the officer posted a message, *"Here is the father holding his son. The son has on what appears to be gang attire."*

I was infuriated! How can you put a stigma like that on a child? The child is about a year old and has no knowledge of what gang attire would be.

I felt like the officer was trying to say my son's death was *gang-related*—which is what police attribute to a large percentage of deaths for young black men.

However, what police don't do is thorough research of a matter. They tend to come to their own conclusions about a matter, and it sticks with them, whether right or wrong. They never posted the truth about what happened to my son. His death was not gang-related.

Your perception of people doesn't necessarily reflect who they really are or what they will become. What I know is that all young men aren't in a gang, and most are just trying to make it to live another day. Some of my children's best friends were in a part of town known for gangs, and young men weren't allowed in that part of town unless they were a part of that sector of people.

My son came to me many years ago and asked, "Why can't we go to see our friends in that part of town?" I explained why. He proceeded to say, "I am going to come up with a name and act like we are in a gang so we can go see our friends in that part of town. We are not in a gang, but they will think we are and leave us alone." That is what they felt they needed to do, and they did just that, and they all stuck to their plan. It became a real thing to the police, and that is how they began to classify them. However, the real truth was it was so they could move about the city and see their friends.

Children Don't Always
Do the Right Things

I've been told that hindsight is twenty-twenty, and looking back, I see where you may train up your children in a certain way, but they might go contrary to what they've been taught. They latch onto and pick up bad habits and the ways of their friends and other people. The people they end up attaching themselves to and their ways are enticing so much so that your child or children will go contrary to what they have been taught. So they might end up conforming or transforming to the ways of other people because it's exciting to them.

My child wasn't perfect, and he'd gotten caught up in a few things in his younger days, so I can see how my husband fell for Miss Deceitful's lies because of what the children used to do.

Life carries the same challenges for people every day, learning to lie, cheat, and steal. Going against everything they have been taught, getting caught up in the midst of foolishness and ignorance they have picked up from other people, and being young, you do foolish things.

For childhood and youth are vanity. (Ecclesiastes 11:10 KJV)

However, if you ever hear someone say, "My child would never do something like that," and many people believe they have perfect children that never do anything wrong. My suggestion to you is, don't believe it or watch out.

You also have people sitting in high places passing judgments on your children. They frown and look at them like they are the scum of the earth, trying to make your child feel small, all while they are paying someone or making a phone call to keep theirs from having a stain on them or a record.

We were all once full of ignorance and folly. We have made many errors ourselves.

People of the world will do a lot of foolish things to have worldly possessions. Desiring to have things they feel they cannot acquire on their own. They will use many methods to take what someone else has, and they will take the life of someone to have what that person has worked so hard to obtain. Just to gratify their flesh, even if it's short-lived.

Don't ever give up on your children! Even when they are doing bad things. Keep praying for them and believing that they will turn around. Sometimes we get angry with them and want to throw in the towel and turn our backs on them. The very children you give up on and turn away from can turn around and surprise you with their achievements.

Your mess might end up being your ministry!

> *But we are all as an unclean thing, and all our righteousness are as filthy rags. None of us are perfect as much as we think we might be, we all have faults.*
> (Isaiah 64:6 KJV)

The world may see your children as dung but see your children like God sees them as precious in his sight.

Paying for Nothing

The insurance I was paying for through the company I worked for was denied. Why pay for something that gets snatched away when needed?

My claim for AD&D insurance. This money was taken from my check every two weeks, and your child could be on the insurance until a certain age. He fit the criteria until his death. They found every reason in the book not to pay that claim.

They did pay out a small life insurance policy, but I wanted to give it back to them because they acted like they were doing me a favor. Hell, I paid to have it!

I called the insurance company to submit a claim, but the representative immediately said, "*You're not entitled to all that money, and you will not get that money.*"

I was flabbergasted! But I put in the claims and was sent a letter stating he didn't qualify for the benefit. It's amazing how he qualified for the benefit when they were taking the money from my checks. Even when you have insurance through your job, they never provide you with a policy to see what's written in their policies or shall I say, their hidden codes for not paying.

Thank God for *a ram in the bush*; I had my children in another insurance policy that paid out immediately. Also, L&I paid because his death was by homicide.

Funeral services are expensive, and one door may have closed, but God opened up another, and all the costs were paid for in full. And I was too weak to fight with those people.

The Most Intense Pain I Had Was Planning a Funeral
Fear Had Taken Hold of Me

Several days went by before my sister had me get dressed to go out to find the things needed to clothe his body for his funeral. Every step was so hard, and I felt weighed down by an unearthly weight, an agonizing pain that I just could not shake.

We found all the necessary items needed to take to the funeral home.

All I knew was that I wasn't sure how I was getting from one place to another. I felt like a hollow shell, and my body was moving, but nothing was in it. I felt as if the largest vacuum in the world had sucked all the life out of my soul. I didn't know how anything was getting done, but everything seemed to be in place.

I was overtaken with fear by day and especially at night. I became afraid. If I wasn't asleep from crying mostly all day and half the night, I was scared. I didn't want to look outside of the doors or windows. I was just afraid, and I felt like I was held hostage by fear unless someone was right there with me. I wasn't sure about anything because my son was shot, and we still had no idea what had happened. Fear followed me, and I was a nervous wreck. As long as someone was near me while I was awake, I felt somewhat safe. I told no one how frightened I was.

One day, I happened to be outside with my husband and my son, and the sun was very bright, and you know how you can see the sunrays in the distance, and it looks like water? I saw an image of a man on my porch moving around as if it was the spirit of my son. I was a fragile mess, and feeling childlike in my mind, I didn't know how to extricate myself from this prison of fear. I asked my son if he saw the image of a person on the deck, but he asked me, "What are you looking at?" Because he did not see the image I was seeing.

The Day of the Funeral
Reflections

I don't remember how I got dressed or again where my husband, daughter, or grandson were. I'd lost sight of them; I don't even remember who drove me to the service. When we arrived, I remembered seeing his dog (Pe-te'), and I cried because the dog looked like he was in as much pain as I was.

Although I had family all around me, I felt so alone. We entered the service, and I couldn't have been alone, but I remember seeing Bishop Drayton, his godfather, and cousin, they were the ministers on the roster. My sister said to me, "God said to listen to the words," as they gave an opportunity for people to come up and speak a few words about him.

The bishop said, "This young man has preached his own funeral, look at all the nationalities of people he has brought together, and both floors packed with just as many standing and waiting outside.

His godfather said, "Bless the Lord, oh my soul, and all that is within me, bless the Lord's holy name."

His cousin said to all who were there, "It doesn't matter who you are or where you came from, we will love the (hell) out of you."

What they said was okay, but what stuck with me were the words of the next few speakers. These were their words:

A young lady said, "I used to be homeless, and your son would come downtown every day where the homeless people were, and he would always tell me how God has a plan for my life, that it's not about being on the streets or homeless. God has something better for you." She continued with how she'd lost everything, even her children to drugs and alcohol. "He told me that if I trusted God, he would bless me to get my life together and get my children back. He kept telling me that over and over."

Then she said, "I hadn't seen him for quite some time, but I heard he'd passed away."

She had to come to the service because she wanted people to know how he encouraged her, how his words made her want to change her life, how she began to trust God and got back on track with life, got a place to live, and ended up getting her children back.

Another young lady came up and said he introduced me to God. She said to me, "You may not know this, but your son was a Bible thumper." Two years earlier, my five-year-old son fell out of a three-story window in Seattle and died, and your son happened to be in the area. He came and said to me, "Look at him." He made me look at him. He said, "He doesn't have a scratch on him, look at him. God just took his spirit, and his body fell out of the window because he needed a reason to leave the earth, it was his time." She said, "At that moment I began to believe that there was a God and to believe in God because he didn't have a scratch on him anywhere, so what else could it have been except God lifting his spirit from his body?"

An old man said, "He used to come by my apartment, and he was always happy and smiling. If I was sick and feeling down, it seemed like he would show up. I was at the store one day, and he said, I'm going to come by and pray for you, he always blessed me."

There were so many speakers that I can't remember them all. When he was a small child, we knew he was going to be a preacher, and we were looking for him to preach in the pulpit. But how soon did I find out that God's plan is always greater than we think? While we were waiting for him to come inside to preach, he was already outside preaching!

> Jesus said to his servants, *Go out into the highways and hedges and compel them to come.* (Luke 14:23 KJV)

Everything They Said Was Good, but *No Words* Could Mask My Pain

Life is not always the way we think it should be. We live our lives wanting our children to take the path we think is righteous, but in reality, it is their life, and they have to make their own path.

He lived a fast life, going and coming and making new friends everywhere he went. And if there was a camera close by, his words were, "Come on and take this picture right quick," as if he was leaving people fragments of himself to remember him by. It's amazing how you never think about these things until it's over. But the Lord let me know some people come into this world, and they live a fast life, and we don't like it because we are one-way thinkers. They are getting around in a hurry. Because they know they don't have long in this world, they are doing all they can do before they get out of here.

An example: would be Black Mamba—Kobe Bryant. He came into this world, faced some challenges, and made an everlasting impact in this world. He did what he had to do before he got out of this world. Better yet, he lived his life and made mistakes while doing it.

You know people love you when you are doing well, but the minute you begin to do bad, they turn and walk away without trying to help you or find the root cause of what is going on in your life. They pass judgments on you and put you down.

You know, like Whitney Houston. As long as she was cranking out hits, everyone loved her, but she was overtaken in a struggle, her audience turned their backs on her. Another one would be Anna

Nicole Smith; even in her struggle, they laughed at her, but as long as she was making money on national TV, as high as a kite, people didn't care because she was bringing in money.

Was there ever any intervention for either of them to get them the help they really needed? Yes, there were, but sometimes habits are hard to break or let go of, and you keep spiraling out of control.

Money isn't evil, the love of money is evil. It causes people to do horrible things, such as lying, cheating, stealing, and killing.

It reminds me of a song I wrote years ago called "Vanity."

Some of the lyrics were the following:

I know that you've been holding on to so much pain,
your passion for worldly things, it seems you cannot gain.
Money, houses, cars, possessions that's your aim,
but these very things can cause you so much pain.
Vanity, its vanity, oh Lord, what's the reason?
Vanity, vanity, can even lead to treason.

Life is filled with challenges. Along with ups and downs, some we will overcome, and some will overtake us.

> *For the love of money is the root of all evil: which while some coveted after, they have erred from the faith, and pierced themselves through with many sorrows.*
> *But thou, O man of God, flee these things; and follow after righteousness, godliness, faith, love, patience, meekness.* (1 Timothy 6:10–11 KJV)

Reflecting back to when he was a child, he was loved by all, and he just had a different spirit. He was drawn to water, and he would play in the water all night until he got sleepy. If you asked him a question during the day, he'd always look up in the sky like he had to wait for someone to give him an answer before he would answer your question.

It took me back to when they were small children, and we were all sitting around upstairs having a discussion about life and what they wanted to become or do when they got older and how many children they wanted when they grew up.

Each child said what they wanted to become or do, and his vision stood out because I remembered him standing in the window and looking up at the sky as if someone was talking to him. The sun was beaming brightly through the window, and we were wondering why he had his face in all that bright sunlight. But as he was looking into the brightness of the sun, he said, "I'm going to have a boy."

He turned around and looked back into the sun again and said, "And a dog. And my son is going to live with you every day, Mama."

We all laughed because he said it as if someone was telling him to say it. I said, "You must be crazy, I'm trying to get rid of you guys!"

So I paid him no mind when he said that at that time. But lo and behold, he had a boy and a dog.

His boy has been with me every day since he was two days old from the hospital. And he had a dog he raised from a puppy that he could hold in one hand. I realized that it was a prophecy that I dismissed when he spoke it. All his growing-up years, no matter how dark or dim the room was with other people feeling down on their luck, as soon as he'd walk into the room, the whole atmosphere would change, like a bright light was turned on. He carried that spirit everywhere with him. He could walk to the store, and people would follow him home, wanting to meet him. He brought us joy.

It's like the world stopped when he was murdered.

If going through his death wasn't agony enough in and of itself, now, I have to go through the trials and sentencing of the young man that killed my son.

There Was No Care in the Room

We went through three attorneys. The first one was a highly-regarded prosecutor that I really liked because he was going to prosecute everyone involved in my son's murder. But all of a sudden, he was removed from the case and was in the news for using racial slurs in previous cases.

The second prosecuting attorney didn't seem to care much about the case. He said, "I guess I can prosecute this case, but I am not sure." I think it was too convoluted for him. I am quite sure most lawyers are like that, but people need you to at least act as if it matters. A short time later, I was advised that he was off the case because he moved.

Then the third and final prosecutor didn't give a rat's behind. He was just as uncaring as the previous one. He said to me, "I'm not worried about all the rest of the people and what they did to cause this. I am just going after the shooter. Whether they were involved or not, I am not dealing with them."

At that moment, I felt "*wow*," my son is just a *blank slate* to him. No matter the words you spoke to him, he might have heard me, but I knew he wasn't listening.

Since I've had time to mull over it myself, I can see that you would have to remove yourself from all the foolishness that had taken place before the incident transpired.

All I wanted was for him to act like he cared or it mattered, but I got nothing.

Meanwhile, I got a call from the first prosecuting attorney, and he said to me, "Your son lost his life behind a lot of foolish people.

He did what any man would do, and that's to protect his house and family. It's a shame that the people around him started all this foolishness and that they woke him up with all their foolishness. He got up to protect his house, he went outside to ready himself to take the heat away from the house, thinking he would have a better angle at the perpetrator before he arrived, but he was too late. They were closer than he thought, and they began spraying bullets with that AK-47." He said, "I don't think that man intended to kill your son, but he wanted to scare the hell out of those girls because of what they did by stealing his stuff."

Quite some time had passed by now, and just before sentencing, we got a call from a court-appointed person for our family. She asked if we wanted to come to court and have words to say regarding how I felt toward the person that shot and killed my son.

Before I wrote anything, I thought it through and said to myself, "*It's easy to say foul things to a person*" of how you feel and all the hateful things you could say.

We only showed up for his sentencing.

So here we are in court with an attorney that's just there to collect a paycheck.

Therefore, I just listened to the proceedings. Being in court listening to everything was like my son being murdered all over again. I did not go to most of the court hearings. And I wouldn't allow my children to go either because there was so much confusion surrounding his death that it was baffling, and we still had no answers.

The shooter's family got to talk and present his case from their standpoint. They said every positive thing they could think of about their son, brother, uncle, nephew, etc., hoping that he would get as little time as possible.

Listening to them and all the things they were saying, I was thinking, "*If I were in their shoes, I would probably say the same things, whether it was true or not.*"

I felt like a penny waiting on change. You get nothing back from that transaction. I watched as the judge and the perpetrator's attorney went back and forth; meanwhile, ours said nothing. When their attorney finished speaking, it was our turn, and our attorney said a few meaningless words. Then the judge asked me if I had anything I wanted to say or read. I said yes.

Even before I wrote out how I felt, I remembered I did not want to be negative. I said to the Lord, "*I can be negative, but I want to give them something to challenge their way of thinking.*"

I wrote what I wanted to say at home, and my husband asked me if I was sure I wanted to say that, and I told him yes. I mustered up what little strength I had and walked to the microphone.

With my husband and sister by my side, I began to read what I wrote, but my tears would not allow me to see the paper it was written on, so I spoke from my heart instead. However, I was resolved to say things that would hopefully challenge their way of thinking. And I spoke from my heart.

I said to him and his family, "I have sat here and listened to all the wonderful things you had to say about your son, brother, friend, father, nephew, uncle, etc."

"My son was also filled with loving kindness. Charismatic."

"He never met a 'stranger,' he was a friend to all people he encountered. He'd help you in any way and would give you anything you needed if he had it to give."

"Being young, you don't really think about what you do or how your actions may affect someone else. All you are thinking of is yourself at that moment. You may not have killed my son with an intention to harm anyone. But did you even think, for even a moment, that there was a possibility that someone may get hurt."

"But your anger toward someone else caused you to do what you did. Now I am left without my son. And my grandchildren are without a father."

After saying how I felt, I looked at him and his family and remarked on their words about him and said to them these words:

At the end of this day, when the gavel comes
down for your sentencing, they will call it justice.
But I say, where is the justice?

Because, when this is over, I can't go to the grave and tell my son, "You can get up now and come home, it's over."

You see, I go to work every single day. I am a taxpayer. Where you're going is a known fact you get "three hots and a cot," three hot meals and a cot to sleep on. All the while, you get to watch TV, pump iron, laugh, and have fun, and I have to pay for it.

I see it like it's a vacation for you to go meet family members you've never met before or haven't seen in a while.

My son won't get the chance to hold his children's hand or take his children for walks in the park and bike rides or brush his daughter's hair, or do the things a father does for his children. Where is the justice in this? Nevertheless, I forgive you, I forgive you, I forgive you!

When I finished, his attorney got back up and said, "After that, I have nothing else to say."

Then the judge said, "After hearing this mother's heart, I wish I could add more time to your sentence, but I can only give you the maximum of ten years, and today this is what you are going to get."

I felt no relief. He was still free to enjoy many pleasures of life. Meanwhile, I have to pay for it because I'm a taxpayer.

A prison sentence is not a punishment, it's a joy ride. He gets to live in a hotel called "prison" with room service.

I will never understand how that punishment fits the crime. You get to enjoy life, laugh about what you did, you get to call your friends and family on the phone, and you only have *temporary travel restrictions*. But you do get to go outside, whether to work or have fun. You get to see another day.

Another Battle

Nevertheless, the clock keeps ticking. Now we are faced with trying to get custody of my grandson, all while grieving the loss of my son.

For support, one morning, my family and I went to my spiritual mom's house, and we began to talk about death. She began to speak, and these were her words to us, "I believe we were all spirits up in heaven with God, and he asked each one of us how long do we want to go to the earth and stay?"

She said, "I think some of us said, one second, one minute, one hour, one day, five years, ten years, fifty years, eighty years. You get what I mean, and none of us knows what we signed up for." We were like spirits floating around in heaven, and when we came to earth, we didn't realize all the things we had to endure. But the Bible says:

> *Many are the afflictions of the righteous, but the Lord will deliver us out of them all.* (Psalm 34:19 KJV)

While we are here on this earth, we are going to suffer some things that we have no control over. As the day lingered on, her words gave me some relief. Her words lifted my spirit, if only for a moment.

By this time, I had to gear myself up to go back to work, which meant I had to ready myself to catch the bus and encounter people on the bus, going and coming from work. Every day on that bus, I could hear the Lord talking to me.

In my head, I kept saying, *"Lord, that is so good what you just said, I should write that down,"* but I was too weak to even do that.

Day after day, the Lord was speaking to me, and I wanted to write down all those things because I felt they should be in a book somewhere, but my hands were shaky. I managed the bus because it was my escape from people feeling sorry for me and me feeling sad.

At work, I was so withdrawn from everyone because the minute anyone said anything to me, I would burst into tears. Although, I managed to do my job. I lost myself in my work to keep from having anything to say to the people around me.

While at work, someone asked me, "*What happened?*" I broke down, and I screamed and teared up so much so that someone from another unit came and escorted me outside of the building in an effort to comfort me.

This was a person I had no idea would stand with me and support me the way she did, and at that moment, I really needed that support. It was hard to go back to work after about two weeks because the pain was still fresh. But I managed to pull myself together enough to go back to work.

I was in a place called "Lo-debar," a low place with no words or communication.

As time went on, another person from the job drew close to me. We began to go on walks every day, and I remember one day, I couldn't contain myself while we were walking, and we found a place to sit. As we sat there, I began to pour out my heart to her, and she stayed the course with me until I was able to gather myself together, and we walked back to work. It so happened my boss was around and caught sight of what happened and told my friend that he was glad she was there with me.

I had no appetite. I lost a lot of weight, but I drank lots of water. Then there are times when people closest to you will hurt you. My brother came by to sit and talk to me and asked me, "*Why wasn't I eating.*"

He said, "*You got to eat something to keep your strength up,*" and "*You might as well accept it because your son is never coming back! So you might as well pull yourself together and start eating and get your strength back.*"

I felt this was the end of life as I knew my son, and he knew me; I will never get to hear him say, "*I love you, Ma,*" or "*Ma, I love you, girl.*" He would tell me, "*Don't let things get to you like that, it ain't that serious.*"

Then I thought about heaven—will we know each other again? Then I heard the spirit of the Lord say to me:

Then shall I know even as also I am known. (1 Corinthians 13:12)

And I thought, *Wow, when I get to heaven, he will look up and say, "Hey, Ma!" and we would embrace.*

Then I said, "Hmm." Then I heard the spirit of the Lord say to me, "*When I called Lazarus from the grave, he knew everyone as he had previously known them when he was living.*"

But I was still hurting. All I could hear was, "*He ain't never coming back!*"

I got so angry with my brother, thinking, *How can he say this to me?* Although I knew he meant well, it was either how he said it or how I received it. All I know is that it hurt like hell, and I didn't want to talk to him anymore. He sat at the table with me and said, "I'm going to sit here until you eat something," but I couldn't do it; I just couldn't do it.

All I know is that I was plenty upset with him, knowing full well what he said was true, but he didn't have to say it.

Shortly after that, my youngest son came over to visit me, and the first thing he said was, "*What is it, Mom? You won't eat anything, and you are going down. What! You don't love us? The rest of your children? Are you just trying to die? What about the rest of us?*"

I wasn't trying to die or be as weak as I was, I was just in a place I knew not of, and I could not explain it, nor did I have the strength to do anything about it.

In this life we will face hardships, but we have to keep our heart with all diligence; for out of your heart flows the issues of life. (Proverbs 4:23 KJV)

This scripture is undeniably true, and there will be many issues in this life.

My sister came a few days later and did church with me in the house a few times, and it was good, but the connection was not there. I thought about trying to go to church, but I couldn't muster up the strength.

I heard the devil say to me, "*You mean you want to go to church and serve God, and he let your son get killed?*"

I had to turn and speak to him and tell him, "*Devil, you have nothing to offer me except death, hell, and destruction, why would I turn my back on God and serve you?*"

I had been active in church, but I could not find the strength to go. I couldn't even find the strength to say my prayers, and I didn't even know what to say to the Lord. I lost a large part of me. I didn't even know where my husband, youngest daughter, and grandson were, but that is how out of it I was in my season of discontent.

On a daily basis, my children seemed nonexistent, nor did I know who had come and gone from my house or even my sister coming in from another state. I don't remember her being anywhere in close proximity to me. Again, I call it "*Lost in Space*" or "*Lo-debar.*"

One day, I began to face the thing I dreaded and began to read the cards that I had received. It took about three years for me to begin reading the cards that were sent to me, but I couldn't bring myself to read them earlier. The sting of my son's death was too fresh. I never wrote a thank you card to anyone because I still couldn't own my pain, and it was so overwhelming.

The outpouring of love from the hearts of so many people began to bring me joy. I began to see the beauty in the cards and grasped the fact that most of them were sent with a heavy heart as well. It was the joy of knowing he touched so many lives and nationalities of people, old and young.

The first year of my son's death date, I stayed home from work and the wells of my eyes were consumed with tears all day.

In the second year, the same thing, and my sister happened to stop by to check on me. She had a feeling I would be home. We talked for a while, and she went on her way.

In the third year, I stayed home on his death date. I happened to be in the garage, and there were many Bibles lying around, so I picked up the one closest to me and opened it. I looked down and began to read, and this scripture came alive in my soul.

> *My frame was not hidden from You when I was made in secret, when I was woven together in the depths of the earth. Your eyes saw my unformed body; all the days ordained for me were written in your book before one of them came to be. (Psalm 139:15–16; NIV)*

I slammed the Bible shut and began to say, "*Okay, God.*" This was going to happen before he began his life with me. And the spirit of the Lord said, "*He was with me, remember before he was, he was with me.*"

This is the passage of scripture that gave me the strength to get up and begin to live again. And I said, "Okay, God."

So when people say, "*It's not going to happen on my watch.*" The fact remains that "their watch" doesn't have anything to do with this life.

Strange as it may be, throughout the entire time of my grieving, I felt like the Lord had me wrapped in a cocoon, and when it was time, I felt him release me. It was like I could see it in the spiritual arena. He was holding me in his arms like a small child, and when it was time to let go, he gently put me down to do it alone.

I felt him let me down from his arms and give me a pat on the backside and say, "*You've got to learn to walk again on your own.*"

At that moment, I became so afraid, and I asked the Lord, "*Why are you doing this to me? Why are you letting me go? I need you.*"

I remembered feeling abandoned by God, and I could not believe he was releasing me to stand alone.

I Was Never Alone

It seemed that during the lowest and most painful times in my life, when I felt all alone and that no one cared, I would share with my friends what I was going through, and they would always say, "You *can handle it, you know what to do.*"

I would get so frustrated with them and walk away asking myself, "*Why should I expect them to care about me and my troubles?*" I didn't know why they had nothing to pour into me, and then I realized it was not their battle, it was mine and mine alone to trust God to help me resolve.

A few years later, I was still upset and angry with my husband because of the words he'd spoken that night after leaving the scene of the crime. His words struck me so hard that I was barely managing with everything else and that, too, was a big part of my hurt. I couldn't hug or connect with him the way a wife should, but I managed to handle being around him.

But there was nothing good in being around him. I just didn't like him at all anymore. So I thought I would go to church. I had one sole purpose in mind, and that was so they could tell me I had grounds to divorce him. I asked my husband if he would go to church with me, and he was glad to do it, but he did not know why I wanted him to go to church with me.

My heart was heavy, my spirit was low, and all I wanted was to be free of my husband. He'd said the worst thing ever to me, and he didn't listen to me. He listened to someone else's words instead of mine even though I told him she was a habitual liar. He wasn't treating my grandson the way I thought he should have treated him.

He just couldn't do anything right in my eyes, and I wanted out of the marriage.

Well, we got to church, and I wasn't listening to anything that was being said by the minister. I was only waiting for them to do the altar call for people to come up for prayer. The time came; the call was made, and I asked him to go up with me, and he did. Before I could tell the minister what I wanted the prayer for, he began to say, "You need to pray for your husband, he never meant to hurt you. He was hurt like you were hurt, and he didn't know what to say, and he prayed for me instead."

What do you know? I was madder than a wet hen! I hated that I went to Church and was mad as hell when he told me to pray for my husband. That wasn't what I wanted to hear, and who is he to tell me to pray for my husband? I said, *"I shouldn't have gone to church in the first place, who does he think he is, telling me to pray for my husband?"* I was mad for about a week or so then I began to pray for him since I know prayer changes things.

God is so amazing in his power and authority. When all else failed, he brought this scripture to my mind:

> *My grace is sufficient for you, for my strength is made perfect in your weakness. Most gladly therefore will I rather glory in my infirmities, that the power of Christ may rest upon me.* (2 Corinthians 12:9)

I had to realize that my weakest point was when I had the most strength because I had to trust in God's Word. And in my trusting and holding on to the scriptures, I gained strength. It never feels good to the flesh to endure hardships, but sometimes God takes you down to lift you up.

Slowly but surely, when I began to pull myself up again, I went back to church. Before that, there was what I thought was a cleansing of myself with moaning and groaning and wanting to be free of the feeling of anger I was holding onto when I saw people that I felt created the chaos that caused the death of my son.

Forgiveness

One night, I got a phone call from my sister asking if I wanted to attend church with her. I asked, "What church are you going to?"

She said, "Pastor Jack's."

I said, "Yes, it would be nice to go to a place where no one knows me."

When we got there, the speaker was on the floor talking to the people at the service. All of a sudden, she said, "The Lord told me to change my message."

She began to speak on forgiveness and how she was going from place-to-place ministering, and one day, the Lord spoke to her about forgiving her father and how she'd held on to the things he'd done when she was a young girl and how she held it against him. The Lord told her she needed to ask him to forgive her for her thoughts and how she felt. She went on about the things he'd done, but at the end of her message, she said, "If anybody got anything in their heart they need forgiveness for, come up to the altar for prayer. I want to pray for you."

Well, nobody moved, and everyone stayed seated. Then she paused for a minute and said, "I tell you what, everybody come to the altar." There were about twelve people there. First, she began to pray with the minister and his wife.

I was next in line, so she grabbed both my hands and said, "Name your children." I did, and she said, "Name them again," so I did. She said, "God said, 'It's that second one.' God said, 'You got to forgive them and release them,'" and she kept repeating, "God said, you got to forgive them and release them."

My pain was still fresh, and I was screaming and hollering. Also, not sure how I ended up on the floor, kicking, screaming, and hollering. She got down on the floor to my level with a towel in her hand—speaking to me, "When your son gave his life to God, God did not take it back. The Lord said, 'Touch this towel that's in my hand as if you were touching the hem of his garment.'" Again and again, she said, "When your son gave his life to God, God said, 'He did not take it back,' but you got to forgive them and release them." After a while, I remember saying, "Okay, God, I forgive them, and I release them to you." After a while, I was able to get up off the floor.

I saw my sister and walked over to where she was and said, "I have probably scared these people to death with my screaming and hollering. It was like all the pain and anger was being released."

She said, "They need to be scared." This is what happens when God is working on you and in you to free you from the chains that have you bound and holding you down.

A few minutes later, the minister came over and spoke to me and said, "God wants you to leap for joy!" And the spirit of the Lord hit me, and I began to dance and shout before the Lord; I truly felt free! That night ended on a great note for me!

However, the process was not complete.

About a week or so later, I found myself asking God, "Did I really forgive them and release them? Did I, God?" Because that night at church, I felt like I had forgiven them, but I really wasn't sure if I had or not. I happened to be in my laundry room, and I asked God again, "Did I really forgive them and release them? Because I was still angry with the people involved in my son's murder." As I was folding my clothes, I heard the spirit of the Lord say to me, "*If I can forgive you for the very thought you had of not wanting your own seed, who are you that you can't forgive them?*"

God took me so far back into the recesses of my mind and brought up something that took place with me about thirty-five years back. He reminded me of when I was in a heavily abusive relationship with my children's father and pregnant. The abuse was so intense that I'd rather not have the child I was carrying than have my child endure being abused while carrying my child and being beaten all the time; I did not want to put my baby through that torture.

I remembered that moment when I said, "God, I don't want this baby!" because I thought he was going to kill me and the baby, and I did not want the child to experience any of my pain. I knew my child could not take that kind of beating or abuse I could barely stand myself.

In my fear and ignorance as a young adult in an abusive relationship, being punched and kicked like crazy, I slept with a gun at my head every night. If I went to the store by myself, I was timed and had to be checked upon return. I feared for myself as well as my unborn child. So I thought that was best; that way, the baby would not have to suffer through the violence.

A little while after my rejecting my own seed, I had a miscarriage about three months into the pregnancy.

God took me back into the recesses of my mind. He brought up the image of that very moment to the forefront of my consciousness. He allowed me to see that I was no better than the people that had done this cruel thing to my child. After all, I had rejected my own seed.

I forgave my husband for all the anger I had toward him and for wanting a divorce. He has been a pillar for my grandson, treating him like his own blood seed. I am grateful that God brought me to myself, and today we have a wonderful relationship with our children and our grandson.

Coming to Grips with Myself and Others

Herein lies the place where I began to accept what happened to my son and move forward. Others depended on me, such as my grandson, my children, my husband, and grandchildren.

I remembered this scripture:

> *For the word of God is quick, and powerful, and*
> *sharper than any two-edged sword, piercing even to*
> *the dividing asunder of soul and spirit, and of the*

*joints and marrow, and is a discerner of the thoughts
and intents of the heart.* (Hebrews 4:12 KJV)

That scripture had been tucked away so tight that I'd forgotten all about it.

I know God is amazing because he allowed me to see myself through a spiritual lens. I realized that I was no better than the people I did not want to forgive. Although I didn't abort, I still rejected my seed. However, the more I prayed, the more I found myself being released from that prison of fear I'd been in for some time. Then one day, I realized it wasn't there anymore.

A reckoning came over me, and I realized that I am a sinner saved by grace. How can I want God's forgiveness for myself and not for them or others? I found myself asking God to forgive me for my thoughts.

*So shall my word be that goeth forth out of my
mouth: it shall not return unto me void, but it shall
accomplish that which I please, and it shall prosper
in the thing whereto I sent it.* (Isaiah 55:11 KJV)

He sent his word to me through the speaker that night, but the process was not quite complete. At the appointed time, he accomplished in me what he sent his word to do, that was to forgive them and release them. Now, I find myself praying for them and their families.

You've Got to Get Up after a Big Fall

God took me down low, and he brought me back up preaching and teaching his word. This gave me an opportunity to reflect back to a few years ago when I was in a place with the Lord that one pastor called having a mountaintop experience, where nothing can touch you. One night before I went to bed, I said my prayers. As I lay there and dozed off to sleep, I felt my spirit leave my body, and my spirit was like a circular ball of matter floating in the atmosphere toward heaven and getting closer and closer to heaven. I remembered how great it felt. It was like my spirit became angelic, and I kept saying, *"Oh God, it feels so good up here,"* as I was traveling further and further toward what I thought was heaven. And saying again and again, *"Oh God, it feels so good up here, God, I would give anything to stay."*

Then suddenly, my spirit returned to my body and shook me. I was awakened and in awe of what had just happened. I got up and sat on the side of the bed facing the mirror and began to touch myself in the face to see if I was alive or real, and I began to poke myself to see if I was still alive.

I wondered if that was what the scripture means when it says the spirit goes back to the creator that gave it. It felt absolutely divine. I could not believe that this experience took place in me, and that was years before my son was murdered. I thought, *If my son felt like that, he'd never want to come back either.*

I remembered my sister saying to me, "God said, 'He's got him,'" and I thought, *What better place?*

I found peace in knowing that his spirit was in the loving hand of my Father, who art in heaven. I experienced the stages of grief that everyone goes through. I was in total shock, thinking, *This was not happening to me.* I can't believe the God I serve would allow this to happen to me with all the things I have had to suffer through already. I even asked God, "*How could you allow this to happen to me? Don't you know that I am your child, and that was my son, he belonged to me.*"

It was as if God replied directly to me and said, "*Jesus was my son, and I gave him for the whole world.*" As I was crying, I could see that the Lord cried too for his son.

And I thought, *He must have felt what I am feeling.*

I was devastated by the atrocity I had faced, but I had reached a higher plane in the spirit. My body was existing but felt like I was walking on clouds all day, and my spirit was in a state of joy unspeakable. Honestly, I thought God was getting ready to take me away from this world, and I was ready. I was in a place with the Lord where I was ready.

My pain was so intense and overwhelming that I could hardly breathe. People kept coming to me to give me cards or say I am sorry for your loss, which only exacerbated what was going on within me. I could not breathe, and it knocked the wind out of me.

I was very angry with the people involved because they were the same people he helped to take care of daily. And they had eaten bread from my table!

I felt like I was angrier with them than the person that murdered my son. If it hadn't been for their foolishness and what they decided to do, none of it would have happened.

After a while, I drew back from people. Anytime anyone said the least little thing to me, I would burst out crying. It was like you could take your finger and touch me, and the tears would come streaming down. My heart was already gripped tight from the pain. Death has a sting that grips so tight you're not sure if you can ever break free.

I thank God for my armor-bearer, my sister, as she was with me every step of the way. She was my voice when I couldn't speak; she stood by me when I couldn't stand. She stayed with me through it all, and I am thankful, grateful, and appreciative for both my sister and my brother, who stood with my husband to help him through the grieving process.

I gave my husband no credit for anything, not once thinking he could be in shock as well or why was he so angry. One day, the Lord let me see that fear, shock, and anger is a part of grief, and he was experiencing what I was experiencing. The Lord spoke to me and said that none of us knew the truth about what happened, and he had been told so many lies about one scenario or another that he didn't know what to think or believe.

Eventually, we got the police report and learned the truth about what happened to my son.

My husband fell to his knees and apologized to me for his thoughts and actions toward me and my sons because so much misinformation had entered his ears, and he believed the lies that were fed to him.

Finally, we got some of the truth about what happened, and the very people that wanted to be around me were involved. Some of these people had been in my home.

I was angry, but God said, "*Vengeance is his, and he would repay.*"

One thing I never experienced was guilt. I had no guilt. I believe that was because I had a great relationship with my son. Well, I can say with all of my children but with him especially.

We would talk about everything, watch movies together, oh what joy! He kept me with a smile on my face, not only me but everyone around him. It was like the minute he walked into a room, the lights would turn on.

That was the spirit he had and carried everywhere he went. I remember when he brought me into his room one day while cleaning, and he had me sit down. He said, "I want to play something for you." He played Boyz II Men—"*Mama, don't you know I love you.*" After the song, he said, "You know you are the hardest-working person I know, and you are the queen of my heart, I love you, Ma!" Every time I hear that song, it takes me back to that day.

Acceptance

I have accepted what happened. I have his oldest son with me, and I am thankful to him for leaving me a part of him. I thank God for the years he gave me with my son. I forgot to mention that he had a set of twins seven months later. He said he wanted more children, but he never got to see the twins.

After being delivered from my anger, I realized how much God loved me. I forgave them and released them, and that freed me.

Now here I am learning how to stand on my feet again and build myself back up in my most holy faith, trusting God for his strength.

It's like I can hear my mother's voice singing in my head, "Grace, God's grace is sufficient for me," and "Walk with me, Lord, walk with me while I'm on this tedious journey, I need you Lord to walk with me".

I told the Lord, "If you want to use me to minister to them, then I need your strength, I'll need to be able to look them in their eyes without hurt, anger, or rage." God has allowed that to be so, not afraid or fearful. I have accepted what happened to my son. Every day I get to see a part of my son through my grandson. And that gives me hope and strength to go on because he needs me, and I have to pour into him the spirit of love and never hate.

When you hear someone say, "*They are not going to let someone die on their watch.*" Their watch has nothing to do with death. When your time is over, it's over. You can't run, and you can't hide.

As a parent, we think our children will live longer than we will. We never want to think of losing a child.

He knew the day was quickly approaching, and he warned me that it was going to happen.

I said to him, "I know," not thinking he was serious. The God I knew wouldn't allow that to happen to me, and I felt it would be my end.

Well, he had spoken the words so clearly, and he said, "Ma, you know how you just know you are not going to make it."

I said, "Yes."

He said, "I'm not going to make it, Ma, I don't mean going back to school or anything like that, that could happen, but that is not what I mean. And don't worry, everybody else will be okay. My youngest brother is going to be something. And you won't have to worry about the rest of them, they will be all right."

I didn't think it was his end, and I thought mine was approaching. I would have traded places with him in a heartbeat, especially seeing my grandson outside playing with all the other children and watching his uncles play with their children. He ran into the house and said, "Mom, can you take me to heaven so I can be with my dad? So he can play with me like everybody else's dad is playing with them outside."

I almost fell to my knees, it hurt so bad to hear those words. And I couldn't get his dad for him, but I know he would have been right there. Then the youngest grandson said, "I'm going to get my dad." They had watched so many videos of their father that they thought he was alive. This is when it hurts when you look at your grandchildren, and there is nothing you can do to help them at that moment in time.

I think of my son often.

A Letter from Him to Me in My Spirit

I can almost hear him reading a letter to me, and this is how it reads:

Mama, remember our time together? We shared many things, joy, laughter, heartache, pain, and even a secret or two. I caused you some grief at times, and you called me a thief. I took this, and you gave me that. We had many spats, and neither one of us liked that, but we always forgave each other. On our mothers, it wouldn't happen again. I lied and stole, let the truth be told, and all the while, you were praying for my soul. I was young and learning, and you gave my backside a good burning.

Over and over, we went round and round, arguing about this and fussing about that. And you kept saying, "Don't let the sun go down on your wrath."

Here you are today, in a totally different way. It may not be what you wanted for me, but this was my destiny. No matter what you or anyone thinks, this day was already planned for me. I'm sorry I left you crying, but this had to be.

You know I loved you, I am your boy as you remember me. I hope it brings your heart much joy. I am thankful I came to know the Lord. And for the time you spent with knees bent, asking God to please let me repent.

I love you, Mama, and thank God for what you meant to me and so many others, but you know all good things must end. Remember what I meant to you and the love we shared that carried us through the good and the bad and all we had, and none of it left you sad.

Don't cry too long, don't see me as gone, continue to worship and praise the Lord through this season you are in, and believe me, this is not the end. Remember, through your pain, God still loves you.

I took heed of how you cried and prayed and watched God answer your prayers. Many days, you taught me well even though I took you through hell, and you never gave up on me.

I did repent; I found true joy. I am so grateful I came to know the Lord. So thank you, Mama, for a job well done. You did what the Lord wanted; you raised a son.

I left fragments of me with you, and I hope my children bring much joy to you.

Mama, there was no me without you, and I am so grateful for all the time I had with you. I didn't mean for this to hurt you, but I know God will see you through this like he has so many other things, and you will make it through.

And remember when you told us when times get hard, this is the prayer to pray:

The Lord is my shepherd; I shall not want.

He makes me to lie down in green pastures: He leadeth me beside the still waters.

He restoreth my soul: He leadeth me in the paths of righteousness for his name's sake.

Yea, though I walk through the valley of the shadow of death, I will fear no evil: for thou art with me; Thy rod and thy staff they comfort me.

Thou preparest a table before me in the presence of mine enemies: thou anoint my head with oil; my cup runs over.

Surely goodness and mercy shall follow me all the days of my life: and I will dwell in the house of the LORD *forever.* (Psalm 23 KJV)

I am pleased to know God gave me you, and remember when God told you that you were created all sophisticated, all hail divine!

It's because you were, and you did for me all that you were supposed to do, and remember to thank God for the time he gave me to share a wonderful life with you.

Forever I will always love my mama, and my love is still floating around you.

Love ya, Ma

My Reply in My Spirit

My letter to him would be as follows:

Forever and always will you be with me throughout all eternity. I miss you every day as if it was the first day I lost you.

In my heart, I know grieving is not what you would want me to do, but still, I grieve because I was stripped of you. Yes, I still grieve because I can't see your smile, your laugh, or talk to or hug you.

I miss the sounds of your voice, your laughter, your charm, and how you held your baby boy in your arms. I tell people there is no expiration date on grief. As a mother, she grieves until her dying day.

Thank you for the fragments of yourself that you left for all to enjoy. Thank you for your children; they bring us great joy. When I'm with them, I see remnants of you, and that gives me hope as I learn to live without you.

You are more than a memory—you're a special part of me. When I look in the mirror, I tell myself that you still live in me.

That hole that was left so deep inside me has been filled with the joy of your children, all three!

You'd be happy to know your brothers and sisters are playing a part in your children's lives. They are always saying they know that you would have done the same if the tables were turned and it was them. They miss you something fierce, and I can say one thing—no one compares to you. We all miss you.

Your children remind me of you, growing up strong, bold, courageous, loving, charismatic, overcoming obstacles, growing into manhood, not backing down from a challenge, and standing tall in the midst of adversity. True to form and who you were, you were everything to so many people. I see the little ones doing things that are reminders of you.

I knew there was greatness in you all your life. You wanted to make things better for others, and the day of the service represented who you were to the fullest. I really did not know you were ministering on a daily basis and walking people through their setbacks, letting them know they can do better to live better and be better. All backgrounds and races were in attendance, and all those old people had so much good to say about you. Even the young spoke in high regards about you.

All I know is nothing is the same since you left us, and there is no greater love than a mother's love. God blessed me with the gift of you, and you blessed the world around you with every good gift God gave you.

I love you, son, and there are many days I still look for you. I pass by the front or back door, and I see images of you, patting your fade with a smile on your face, waiting for me to open the door so you can grace us with your presence or lend a helping hand. I do hold onto what you said when you told me, *"Don't let things get to you like that, let go of the negative people in your life, they mean you no good they keep up strife. You are the hardest working woman I know, and I am thankful that I have a mom like that."*

I miss those compliments and the movie nights. But trust me, your children have walked through that gate, and now we have to watch a movie together; they make me!

Again, your love will never fade from my heart.

Life Can Be Lovely and Gratifying

I have my son's children close around me, and the love I had for my child, I get to pour into his children and all my grandchildren. It's a blessing to know I have a part of him still with me, and as the pages of their lives keep turning, they are beginning to look like him and sound like him. He is ever so near, and I am grateful for the Lord restoring my joy through his children. God has given me beauty for ashes.

Every day I am learning that we can control some things, but one thing none of us have control over is death; it's ultimate, and it has to be. You can't outrun it, and you can't hide from it. When it's over, there is no turning back. It's harsh to us because we have been stripped of someone we loved and cared for, and they are no longer with us. But my son's words when he was preaching to his friends a week before he was murdered, he asked them, "What is the one thing man can't escape?" They couldn't answer because they didn't know what he was talking about. So he told them, "It's death! No one can escape death. We have to learn to live with it and know that it is part of living."

That phone call I got—no one wants to receive a call like that. *It knocked me out without being punched.*

No one is ever ready to receive bad news, and you certainly aren't prepared to handle it. You don't know how you will respond or react to such devastating news. But I can say I have lived the scripture that I grew up reading to my grandmother almost every day.

> *The Lord is my light and my salvation; whom shall I fear? the LORD is the strength of my life; of whom shall I be afraid?*
>
> *When the wicked, even mine enemies and my foes, came upon me to eat up my flesh, they stumbled and fell.*
>
> *Though a host should encamp against me, my heart shall not fear: though war should rise against me, in this will I be confident.*
>
> *One thing have I desired of the LORD, that will I seek after; that I may dwell in the house of the LORD all the days of my life, to behold the beauty of the LORD, and to enquire in his temple.*
>
> *For in the time of trouble he shall hide me in his pavilion: in the secret of his tabernacle shall he hide me; he shall set me up upon a rock.*
>
> *And now shall mine head be lifted up above mine enemies round about me: therefore will I offer in his tabernacle sacrifices of joy; I will sing, yea, I will sing praises unto the Lord.*
>
> *Hear, O Lord, when I cry with my voice: have mercy also upon me, and answer me.*
>
> *When thou said, seek ye my face; my heart said unto thee, Thy face, Lord, will I seek.*
>
> *Hide not thy face far from me; put not thy servant away in anger: thou hast been my help; leave me not, neither forsake me, O God of my salvation.*
>
> *When my father and my mother forsake me, then the LORD will take me up.*
>
> *Teach me thy way, O Lord, and lead me in a plain path, because of mine enemies.*

> *Deliver me not over unto the will of mine ene-*
> *mies: for false witnesses are risen up against me, and*
> *such as breathe out cruelty.*
> *I had fainted, unless I had believed to see the*
> *goodness of the Lord in the land of the living.*
> *Wait on the* Lord: *be of good courage, and he*
> *shall strengthen thine heart: wait, I say, on the Lord.*
> (Psalm 27)

We have to learn how to endure.

My open wound has been somewhat closed; retaliation is not on my mind, and I am thankful that God loved me so much that he wanted me delivered and free from the thoughts running through my mind of avenging my son's death.

Retaliation is not right.

No matter how just or righteous we think it might be, it doesn't change what happened. God said, "*Vengeance is his, and he will repay.*"

It may not be the way you want him to repay, but let the Lord fight that battle for you.

Deliverance Came

I wanted to be free of the feelings I had and the overshadowing anger I felt every day because it was like torment to my soul.

I remembered the scriptures and began to pray the scriptures and tell the Lord, "I am your child, and I cannot serve you with this feeling hanging over me of being angry and not even knowing the truth about what happened to my son."

This scripture came creeping through my mind:

> *The righteous cry, and the LORD hears, and delivers them out of all their troubles.* (Psalm 34:17 KJV)

I had to get real with myself because of the evil thoughts I had in my head, and up pops:

> *Confess your faults one to another, and pray one for another, that ye may be healed. The effectual fervent prayer of a righteous man availeth much.* (James 5:16 KJV)

Then I heard the Lord say to me:

> *And ye shall know the truth, and the truth shall make you free.* (John 8:32 KJV)

To this day, I do not know the full truth about what happened to my son or everything that transpired. Therefore, I decided to let it go because I could not change the results. Also, the truth God wanted me to know about was lying within me. How could I condemn someone else when I, too, am a sinner saved by God's grace? When I rejected my own seed, he forgave me for that very thought I had in my mind.

Today I am living in a state of victory. I know that God still loves me. The hurt and pain I once felt is not so hard anymore, except for the tears I cry from missing my son. A mother will cry until she, too, has been covered in the dirt of the ground.

There will be many afflictions in this life, but God will deliver you out of them all. I try to live my life where I stay in the secret place of the Most High to be under the almighty wings of God.

I am happy to know that God loved me so much that he wanted me to be free from the open wound I had and the anger I felt toward the people that caused the ruckus that killed my son. I think I was angrier with them than the shooter because their actions caused all the commotion.

Today I am free in my inner self and can talk freely with the people that I feel were involved. God reminded me of his love.

> *There hath no temptation taken you but such as is common to man: but God is faithful, who will not suffer you to be tempted above that ye are able; but will with the temptation also make a way to escape, that ye may be able to bear it.* (1 Corinthians 10:13 KJV)

He has shown me that he had a hedge of protection all around me, and no weapon formed against me would prosper.

Food for Thought

On this journey with so many passages filled with trouble and confusion and sometimes great things, life is our greatest teacher as we journey through one pit stop after another. There are many doors to go through, and each one teaches valuable lessons. On this journey we call life, there are passageways we have to take.

Some passageways may begin in a good way, leading you to believe all is well, then you get down the road, and you find there is a fork in the road, and you are confronted with the decision of which way to go.

Other passages may begin bumpy with many twists and turns. But you keep going no matter what, and you are not sure if you are on track or not, nor has thought been assembled in your mind about where you are headed.

Each of us has a journey with passageways we are not sure of, and some will have many snares and traps set up for us. It's like a constant obstacle course that you've got to figure out, and you can't get through the next passageway until you figure out how to get through the one you are in right now.

One never really knows what to do, but you got to go through it because it's what molds and makes you a person.

Some passageways are set up to appear as if you chose correctly, so you keep going through them, and the further you get through the passageway, you find out that this was not the way you wanted to go.

Now you are left wondering what and how in the heck you got caught up being where you are because what's in front of you is not for you, and it's certainly not the place you want to be, so you say to yourself, "*Here I go again.*"

Now, you have to begin again from where you are and hope the next passage is the right one.

This is when you have to dive deep, do some soul-searching, and take inventory of how you got there and what it will take to get out. Because you are coming into the awareness of knowing who you are, what you want, and where you want to be in this life.

Ah, that bumpy passage leaves you wondering, *Am I ever going to get out of here? How did you get caught being in this place?* You realize it was not the journey you wanted to take.

Bumpy passages can be so devastating, and you don't know how to break free, but once in a while, you may get a breakthrough. It seems like as soon as you break free and find refuge, you find that you have to face another trial or tribulation. Once in a while, you go through a season of calm and settled nerves or a resting period before you have to go through another passageway.

I can equate it to being born. We all know how we enter into the world, but we don't know what kind of life or family we will enter into once we are here. Some have good, healthy, nurturing parents to demonstrate love, care, compassion for others, good self-esteem, and everything a person could hope for on their journey.

While others enter into a life of chaos, trouble, confusion, and destruction, barely surviving, messed-up parents, hardly having anything to eat or wear, drugs and alcohol everywhere, no nurturing, no care, children left to raise themselves with no one to help and, the parents forbid you to help them because "they can take care of their own children!"

No matter which passageway you take or enter—your journey is for you and you alone to take. Now the child that grows up with all the necessities in life, and the best of everything in life, you can only imagine how they look down and frown on the child living in chaos.

Even the parents of the well-to-do child don't want their children to associate with the child who's struggling just to get through the day. There are times you can hear the echoes of conversations from parents that are stable or well off, discussing the misfortunes of less fortunate ones.

You can hear them whether they are on the job, bus, train, plane, in restaurants, etc., saying things like, "*I don't want my children associating with the likes of those people,*" and I don't want them to go anywhere near their parents or their children. Never once having a thought of how the less fortunate child may feel or that they may be going through so much pain and anguish.

Parents that are stable give rise to how great their children are, how they may be going to college, are in a successful program or landed a great job. Meanwhile, the less fortunate child may be going back and forth to jail or prison, and what a shambles he has made of his life. We have all heard *he said, she said*, and they won't amount to anything; they are just like their parents, a nobody, a nothing.

How can a child growing up with no structure or care know how to train themselves to do good when it has never been demonstrated to them? When life dictates that you pick up learned behaviors from what is being modeled in front of you on a daily basis. Unless someone intervenes to show a child some love, compassion, kindness, and a lot of it, along with coping skills for how to manage in this world, the child will continue to be left in the dark and maybe never get to know or understand how to overcome struggles, trials, and tribulations.

Sometimes the school of hard knocks comes along to teach a person many things. The old people used to call it "*bought sense.*"

A person figures things out as they go through their journey and face some tough challenges (hard knocks); they realize their ways are not working, so they have to learn new behaviors because what they are doing is not working.

Passageways can be tricky things. Choices have to be made because sometimes a person wonders how a kid that was so great ended up being so messed up. Having problems such as, being drug addicted, alcoholic, prostitute, or murderer. And the very kid you trampled on with your words and misdeeds, that nobody of a kid that you did not want associating with your kid has turned their life around. They became a good person making something of themselves.

Life teaches you how to live. So don't count people out as dung. Pray for them. Just because you grew up with no struggles, trials, or having to make ends meet day-by-day doesn't make you better. You just had a better quality of life. Make no mistake about it; you may be up today, but no one knows where they will end up tomorrow.

All those parents with noses so high in the air with arrogance just because you have nice things just as God blessed you to have it all; it can all be stripped away in a heartbeat—yes! Just like that.

It's easy to judge others when you haven't had to suffer or go through hardships. Every blessing you get is not for you. God allows us to have blessings to test our management skills and also to see if we will help those who are less fortunate.

Remember, some doors God opens for us are not expressly for us. God opens doors for us to utilize what's behind that door to bless others.

Instead of being a selfish thinker, thinking you created wealth on your own, who endowed you with the knowledge, strength, and wherewithal to have the things set before you. Think beyond yourself and your household; surprise someone with a gift of something you know they need—and don't withdraw your hand from those in need and continue to give to those that have.

Extend your hand and give out of the substance you have to those that are truly in need. Robin Hood didn't have it to give, so he stole from the rich to help the poor. But you don't have to do that as it's already in your arsenal to give and to help nurture a struggling child or children.

When children grow up in awkward situations or bad surroundings, don't always take the approach that money is the solution to their problem.

Help is not always throwing money at a problem, but it's in finding a solution to the problem and implementing a plan to make changes for a better outcome. Sometimes a kind word of encouragement will go a long way.

The singer Tupac had a song called "*Me Against the World*."

Sometimes children feel like they are the problem, and the world is against them. As long as you are doing well, people will treat you well. But as soon as you mess up, they'll turn their back on you, mostly blaming the parents of the child for the wrong things the children may be doing or has done.

When in actuality, the parent has taught them right from wrong in all situations and gave them the best upbringing and tools for knowing how to manage and cope with things. How to be respectful? Don't take what's not yours to take, help someone in need, and just be a productive member of society. However, the Bible says, *"Foolishness in bound in the heart of a child."*

Just because a child turns eighteen doesn't mean they are not childlike. Society dictates that they are an adult, but how many eighteen-year-old children do you know that may be eighteen but have the mind of a thirteen-year-old child, still developing and trying to comprehend everyday life?

I remember hearing a teenage boy getting ready to graduate but had a fear of graduating and said, *"I'm not ready for this, I don't want to face what's coming, leaving home to go to college, becoming an adult and living life on my own. I don't think I can take the stress."*

I paused for a moment and began to take an inventory of the people I'd seen and some I know that still haven't grown up. Take a look around you, do a quick scan or survey, and you will see a lot of adults that haven't grown up yet. My children and their friends during their teenage years kept me on my face praying and crying out to God for them.

I had a friend from church to ask the pastor and some of his deacons to intervene, but all they did was talk about me because they had no answer.

But having four boys with each one of them having about five friends for a total of twenty-four. It was hard to keep up with them, but I did and the people in the community weren't so pleasant to any of them.

But they didn't know the struggles these kids were facing. They were so busy with their lovely lives that they looked down on the children in the neighborhood. These kids would ask me, "*Why do they look at us like we got mess all over us?*"

You can explain things to them to the end of the earth and beyond. If they don't know it or understand it, how can they capitalize on it? The life they knew, they didn't think or believe that things could change or that there were any good people in the world.

Then you sit and listen to them telling you why they did and do the things they do. Then you find out it's their way of life, the only way they know.

So I took the initiative to show them love and kindness to tell them about how the life they were leading would continue to take them down a spiraling, out-of-control, dead-end path with no hopes or dreams or ambitions. I told them they had the power to change the narrative of what they felt people were thinking toward them.

Being a survivor of domestic violence myself, running for my life with my children, and suffering the most intense fear I'd ever known. A miserable life that I thought we would never make it out of except through death. But we made it out safely and without harm.

I have to thank God for that, along with a faithful ambassador, Mrs. Bo. She would always tell me, "*I've been praying for you and your children, and God is going to bless you and your children to get away from here.*" She knew the trauma I was going through because she suffered through the same DV trauma with her husband.

Ending up in a state I'd only heard about with children in tow, I had to find my way as a single mother, raising children on my own, beginning with my sister opening her door and allowing us to crowd their space. Learning to be on my own, making decisions without someone telling me what I better do.

I tried to instill in my children good morals and values while doing the best I could to suffice off of what was given to us, along with trying to figure out a plan for my life being alone with children.

The city I was in had access to programs and all kinds of resources for help if you needed it and even crisis lines. Something I'd never heard of.

Every time I thought we wouldn't make it, someone would tell me about a resource that was available to me. I had state assistance for a while and was able to move into housing and have my own place. The assistance was not enough to pay the rent and the bills, and I was crying.

A friend of my sisters came by, and she happened to ask what was wrong. I told her, and she said, "*Oh, they got assistance to help you with that, call this number.*" I did, and they helped just as she'd said.

God had all kinds of blessings in store for us. At the place where we moved to, my sister had a friend around the corner, and she would come over every day. We would speak but never hardly exchange words. I didn't know her; she didn't know me, and we had nothing to talk about, but she would play with my children and pull off their shoes. I just thought she was weird.

I had no idea she was observing to see what we needed. She would leave and come back and bring clothes and shoes for the children, pots, and pans for me. People gave me furniture and blankets; we had everything we needed, and I didn't have to pay for a thing. It was God's goodness in the making and how remarkable it was for me and my family.

As a single mother raising five children alone, everything went pretty well in their younger days. But their teenage years gave me the blues. I grew up when they were growing up. I learned how to stand in the face of adversity, affliction, chaos, trial after trial, not just with my own children but the neighborhood children that leaned on me for strength.

Our lives weren't perfect, and my children were fallible, as we all are (in case you thought you had perfect children). They did many things I did not approve of, but we survived, got off of state assistance, and were able to move into a wonderful home.

Things began to get better, and I thought the chaos was behind us. After all the afflictions I went through, even with the children that were not mine. I cared for other people's children, and God allowed me to endure. Those same children today are adults with their own families, and they have apologized for all the foolish things they did and put me through. Today they are living better lives, and many have told me how much they love and appreciate me. Some of those young men call me Mom. They have said, "*When nobody else cared or stood up for us, you did, and I want you to know I thank you.*"

You see, God told me to keep ministering to all the children and said, "*One may wake up tomorrow and have a revelation of what you are teaching, and one may wake up five or ten years from now and have a revelation of what you have been saying and teaching them because foolishness is bound in the heart of a child.*"

The world may see them as filthy rags and dung and don't think "wayward-out-of-control children" deserve to breathe the air or to live on the earth. That is not how God sees them, keep praying for the troubled youth and teaching them my principles. It's with loving kindness that I have drawn you. You keep being loving and kind, and God will draw them in, but it won't necessarily be in your time frame.

We have a lot of children in the penal system for stealing from the store and doing all kinds of things to get attention. The sad thing about the penal system is there is no help given to the children when they are locked up.

I do feel this is where they need to have intense counseling for children to get to the root cause of what is going on in their lives and have role reversals so they can see themselves and their actions being played out.

Then have the counselors help them with coping skills to learn new behaviors and how to manage when they are released back out into the world. There are so many children filled with hurt, pain, and anger, and most of them just need to feel loved. They don't want you telling them you love them. They need you to show it through your actions. A smile doesn't cost anything. Sometimes, the question "*Are you okay?*" can change the life of anyone.

Only because you took the time to make them feel cared for, and yes! The narrative of a child's life can be changed, and medication is not the answer to every problem. Medication only suppresses hurt and pain, it doesn't deal with raw emotions. Whatever happened to a child just having a "*bad day?*"

And encouraging the child on how to get through it because there will be many battles in everyday life they have to face, and putting a Band-Aid on a cut is not always best. There is a greater problem when children can't have a bad day without being medicated. They learn to deal with nothing. Hmm!

Life is not all about you and your feelings and what you think or believe. I feel we are all here to learn how to live with and be resourceful for one another to lift up your brother or sister when they are down. I don't mean your biological brother or sister because we are all brothers and sisters.

Let the truth be told. Adam and Eve were the beginning of life, and all men and women began from them. When God flooded the world, Noah and seven persons were saved, and they were the bloodline of Adam and Eve, and by that same bloodline, we are here. I haven't read where God made more people, which is why we all bleed red for the blood of Jesus. I am your sister, and you are my brother, so we are one in Christ.

We need to stop berating and casting aspersions on one another and let love resonate in our hearts and mind.

Once in a while, put yourself in another person's shoes. I know we have people that are so privileged that they can't begin to see or imagine themselves in a person's shoes that don't have much of anything.

Who can cast the stone?

* * *

Think not that I am come to send peace on earth: I came not to send peace, but a sword.

For I am come to set a man at variance against his father, and the daughter against her mother, and the daughter in law against her mother-in-law.

And a man's foes shall be they of his own household.
(Matthew 10:34–36 KJV)

The question is, why?

I believe this was spoken so we can learn to live peaceably among each other. It sometimes seems like there is always a ruckus going on, disturbing your sleep, like you can't get a moment of peace in your own house.

It seems someone is always acting like a fool, stealing, fighting, lying, cheating, and addictions, and it always seems to be around you. Here you are trying to live a good life, and chaos is always somewhere close by.

You begin to ask yourself—"*How do I seem to be caught up in the minutiae of someone else's caca?*"

Now since we know that he didn't come to bring peace but the sword, this should automatically tell us that we are going to go through some things in our lifetime. Believe me when I say, your household is not the only one going through difficult things brought about by other people.

The devil uses all kinds of tactics to come against us, but you have to learn the tricks of the enemy. It doesn't matter what trick he uses to come against you as long as he accomplishes his mission. He will use your mother, father, sister, brother, children, and the people that are close to you to turn your world upside down. Once you have been brought to a low degree, the devil has completed his mission; he moves on to the next person.

However, you have to learn the tricks of the devil, so you won't get caught up so easily.

An example: if you have a brother that continues to come to you with his sob stories, "*My baby needs his medication, can I borrow a few dollars? I'll pay you back*" or "*I ran out of gas trying to get to my new job, can I borrow a few dollars? I'll pay you back*" or "*We need food in the house, can I borrow a few dollars? I'll pay you back.*"

Well, if he didn't pay you back the first time or the second time, what makes you think he will pay you back the third time? Then you find out the baby wasn't sick, he had no job lined up, and the children didn't look like they'd missed any meals!

They were all lies. Once you recognize the lie and you see him coming, knowing it will be something else this time, you prepare yourself to ward off the enemy's tactics. So when he comes to ask, you prepare yourself to tell him, "*I don't have it*," because you now realize he is using you to gratify his habits.

But you can't be angry with him for not paying you back. If you keep letting him have the few dollars he asked for, and you're angry because he hasn't paid you back, who should you be angry with—him or you?

If you decide to give away your money or possessions, thinking an addict, liar, or thief will pay you back, think again. Always ask yourself if you have it to give away?

If so, then give it. But if it's going to hurt you when they don't return what they borrowed, don't let it go.

The devil causes people to do all kinds of things to manipulate you. Once you learn to recognize the tricks of the devil coming toward you, ready yourself to ward them off.

It's easy to be angry, but it takes endurance to love in spite of how people treat you or come at you. Remember, learn to recognize the schemes and tricks of the devil.

> *The Lord hath appeared of old unto me,* saying,
> *Yea, I have loved thee with an everlasting love:*
> *therefore, with lovingkindness have I drawn thee."*
> (Jeremiah 31:3 KJV)

Lessons learned the hard way are great lessons.

We are not as perfect as we would like to think we are. So before you want to cast a stone at someone else, examine yourself like the scribes and Pharisees had to.

> *And the scribes and Pharisees brought unto him a*
> *woman taken in adultery; and when they had set*
> *her in the midst,*
>
> *They say unto him, Master, this woman was*
> *taken in adultery, in the very act. Now Moses in the*
> *law commanded us, that such should be stoned: but*
> *what sayest thou?*

> *This they said, tempting him, that they might have to accuse him. But Jesus stooped down, and with his finger wrote on the ground, as though he heard them not.*
>
> *So when they continued asking him, he lifted up himself, and said unto them, He that is without sin among you, let him first cast a stone at her.*
>
> *And again he stooped down, and wrote on the ground.*
>
> *And they which heard it, being convicted by their own conscience, went out one by one, beginning at the eldest, even unto the last: and Jesus was left alone, and the woman standing in the midst.*
>
> *When Jesus had lifted up himself, and saw none but the woman, he said unto her, Woman, where are those thine accusers? Hath no man condemned thee?*
>
> *She said, No man, Lord. And Jesus said unto her, Neither do I condemn thee: go, and sin no more.*
> (John 8:3–11 KJV)

I can only imagine that Jesus was writing things, such as liar, thief, murderer, swindler, fornicator, etc. I believe he was writing every one of their sins on the ground, and when they realized they were no better and they had been exposed and made ashamed by Jesus, they realized, *"How can I throw a stone at this woman and I, deserve to be stoned myself?"* so they dropped the stones and went away.

When Jesus lifted up his head and asked her, *"Woman, where are your accusers? Has no one condemned you?"*

She said no, and he said, *"Neither do I condemn you."*

God allows us to be tempted and tried even unto death to test our faith. It will either draw us closer to him or push us farther away. The enemy pulls us down, but Jesus lifts us up.

Everything he allows us to go through is because he has already made a way of escape for us to get through it.

After all, which one of us can cast a stone at another person? We may be doing okay today, but don't forget to look back at all the times the Lord saved us from the things we got caught up doing, and some of those things could have caused us to be in prison or death. Once we were free from the mess we created and got caught up in, we began to live better and do better.

But only with the help of God.

God does not condemn us, but he convicts us, which is to make us more conscious and aware of our sins or wrongdoing, so we won't keep doing the same things over and over and getting the same results.

Our results are death, hell, destruction, and his result for us is abundant life.

The bottom line is, no matter how you feel or what you see, this whole world is bigger than you and me. We can change things when we stop thinking we are better. We get better by being better and doing better. My request is to give the gift of love and help nurture someone who needs it. Don't forget you have to learn to recognize the schemes and tricks of the devil.

Reality Check

People say a lot of things they have no clue about, such as when they are in charge of someone, they will say things like, "nothing will happen to that person on my watch", then people die.

God told me the world needs a reason. We know how we enter into this world through our mother's womb—giving birth or through a petri dish. But no one knows how they will exit this world!

We ask the question, what happened?

The answer is usually suicide, cancer, heart attack, careened off a cliff, fell 150 feet, got hit by a car, shot and killed, abducted and murdered, or fell from a three-story building.

We need a reason to exit this world. God showed me that before the bullet hit my son, he had already taken his spirit, and he didn't feel a thing. This was my resolve, along with the scripture from Psalm 139:16 *your eyes saw my unformed body; all the days ordained for me were written in your book before one of them came to be.*

Looking to Find Me

When I look in the mirror, I see what I see, my reflection, the very image of what I think is me. I ask myself—is there anything more to me in this image I see reflecting back at me? Am I digging deep enough to find all the hidden treasures that lie within me?

My hopes, my dreams, and my aspirations, is there a possibility that there is something more that I just don't see? How can I tap into the good and well-pleasing things within me that are embedded? The possibilities, inside of me, the true me, stuck within me.

How deep must I dig into the abyss of my soul to find all that lies within me? How many layers of my soul must I unfold to find the hidden beauty within me? I feel something greater is hidden inside of me.

I'll keep digging to find the hidden things that are lying dormant within me, but I still don't know what I see when I look in the mirror at myself.

Now, I know what a diamond in the rough means, so I will keep digging because there is a diamond waiting to be unearthed from the layers of matter within me.

Sometimes you have to dig deep to find the treasures hidden inside of you. They are there, and there are many of them, but you will never know if you don't search for them or activate the treasure.

So the person I see—when I look at me—has many treasures buried inside of me. I may have looked, and I may not have found any treasure today, but I will keep looking because I know greater things are coming my way.

The key to finding some of the greatest treasures of all are the trials you go through and the lessons you learn through each trial.

Evolve

I have been wounded, torn, battered, and beaten, and life has had some battles for me, but I have been strong and courageous, and somehow, the battles didn't defeat me. I found strength from within to overcome what could have been my end. I was able to stand because I had a true friend.

He took me by my trembling hands and lifted my bowed-down head. He walked and talked to me, and at times, he carried me when I could not stand, and he held me up. He gave me more joy than I knew was possible.

I shifted my focus from being a part of the crowd and taking every phone call, and I separated myself and became a crowd of one with my Maker. I let go of the things that were hindering me and stayed on the potter's wheel so he could correct some things inside of me.

We always blame others for our issues and never take the time to investigate or ask the question, are they the problem, or am I my own problem or the reason for the things that are happening to me?

Quit blaming others for your problems, and mistakes and take a long inventory of yourself to see how you are the sole contributor to your mistakes.

Do you ever ask or say to yourself, maybe my problem is me? Define yourself. Who are you? Are you a liar or truth teller? Are you a giver or a taker, offender or defender, like to punch or throw jabs or be punched and take jabs, like to inflict hurt and pain or gentle and loving?

Really, who are you? Everything that happens is not always someone else's fault.

We are all fallible human beings highly capable of getting things wrong and making mistakes.

Take ownership of the person you are, and if you don't like that person—you've got to work on changing that person into the person you would like to see or become.

It is true; you can grow to become a better reflection of yourself that you would like to be. Evolve yourself!

For example, there was a person that was well-known for being a liar; when you would see the person coming or entering, you would begin to hear voices rising from the lips of people with adjectives that had been applied to that person.

After a while, that person left the scene of all those people that knew him that way. Years passed before they saw him again, but when he returned, the people were looking for the same person and using those same adjectives about him. But lo and behold, the people couldn't believe it was the same person. That person went away and worked on changing the image people had of him. He changed the definition of himself.

Someone asked him, "Were you really like that person with all those things people said about you?"

He advised, "I left hurt because I was known as a liar, and I wanted to change the narrative about myself, and I did not want to return because of the thoughts people had toward me. Yet I mustered up the courage to return, and I returned a new person because I did everything I knew how to change the narrative people had about me." He continued, "I evolved."

He became a beacon of light to others. Dark clouds do fade, and the light shines through as day. Who can take your pain away and turn midnights into the day? The night is light to him because he is light, and there is no darkness in him at all.

When the dark cloud is lifted, you begin to see things with new eyes, and a different light appears.

God is light, in Him there is no darkness at all. (1 John 1:5 KJV)

Lift Up Your Head

Hey, you—yeah, you! With the hung-down head.
All the promises that were broken,
All the dreams that didn't come to pass.
Why so downcast?
Hey, you—yeah, you! Thinking you had it all,
And feeling betrayed because it didn't last.
Why so downcast?
What's the matter? How can I help?
You don't have to go around moping and crying when there is help.
He's right there with arms stretched wide,
But you won't turn to him because of your pride.
He's right there he hastens to answer your call,
But you keep bumping into a brick wall.
You won't let go, but you claim you can't take the stress any more.
You call on your friends, and they don't seem to care.
They have no time for you in your despair.
It seems no one cares when you are in a downcast state of mind.
You feel you can hardly bear the hardships that have come upon you.
You must believe that there is someone somewhere that cares for you.
Why so downcast? Don't you know, you are never alone?

All races aren't given to the swift, and all battles aren't for the strong,
You have to believe and hold on,
The greatest race won, and the strongest battle fought is done,
Through the power of prayers and believing God for a change to come.

*The fervent effectual prayers of the righteous
avails much.* (James 5:16 KJV)

Life's greatest battles are fought in prayer, and the race is won by releasing and letting God handle whatever comes your way.

Just a Simple Thought

There are things I can take care of or handle on my own, but when the issue is bigger than me and my strength, I release those issues to God. Who can win a race or fight a battle better than God?

Hopefully, this will help you; God gave this to me back in 1996.

When I thought God made me stupid, I felt like a shell of a person, a nobody.

Always asking God, "Why won't you let me be mean to people like they are to me?"

He gave me these words.

> *I Am Created,*
> *All Sophisticated,*
> *All Hail Divine.*

Horeb—the mountain of God

You will serve God on this mountain.

I *am* has sent me to you; I have watched over you and have seen what has been done to you in Egypt.

I have promised to bring you up out of your misery in Egypt into a land flowing with milk and honey.

Egypt is the place you are caught up in.

Prayer of *If*

Lord,

If I could just hide in a cave and talk to you continuously on my face and come out with infinite wisdom, knowledge, and understanding like Solomon.

If I had the ability to run the race you have set before me with the strength that Elijah had when he out ran Ahab's chariot.

If only I could endure the snarls of bodily afflictions like Job when he had intense pain from the boils that were all over his body.

If I had courage like Caleb when he wanted to conquer another mountain.

If I had the compassion of Moses when he led your people out of Egypt to the promised land, and the people trusted and followed him because they desired something far greater than what they left behind in Egypt.

If I had the strength to fight off the negative when the world comes against me like Noah did when people laughed and ridiculed him for all those years while he was building the ark.

If only I had the faith that Sarah had when you told her she would conceive a child in her old age, and she bore a son.

If I had the courage of that mother that was willing to give up her child to another woman to keep him from being slaughtered or cut into two pieces.

If I had the strength of Abraham to sacrifice or deliver up his only son, Isaac, trusting that God would provide, and there was a ram in the thicket of a bush.

If I had the courage Lot had to leave a city behind that was home to him without looking back and turning into a pillar of salt.

If I had the strength and courage that Sampson had when he cried out to you one last time before he pushed down the pillars of the temple, knowing his own life would be taken when it was done.

If I had the courage of Shadrach, Meshach, and Abednego, when they didn't bow before the king's golden statue because you were their God.

If I could be like Samuel when you called him three times, and he said, "Speak for your servant is listening." Help me to listen when you are calling.

If I could only be true to myself and do what you have called or commissioned me to do because I am not like any of those mentioned, I am just who you want me to be.

Help me to focus on myself and my ability to do what you have called me to do, just as all those before me did what you called them to do. Help me to be strong and courageous in everything I do in my daily walk with thee.

Father, I thank you for your mercies that are new every morning. I've learned if we never have trials, how can we grow? You are an awesome God!

> You walked me through what I believed to
> be the toughest trial of my life, and I thank you
> for never leaving me. Amen.

We've all heard the slogan, "Hurting people, hurt people." This is a true slogan.

People try to avenge the wrong that was inflicted on them by another person. Therefore, by any means necessary, they are going to get them back for what was done unto them.

Not knowing that their actions are getting ready to set off a bunch of catastrophic events, creating a stench in the atmosphere by stirring up chaos brought on by their devious actions. Before you know it, their action has spiraled so far out of control that there is no coming back from it once it begins.

All they know is they want to harm someone or cause harm to their things, never once giving thought to the difficulties that ensue or that the aftermath would be so devastating when it's over.

We were taught as children, "Think before you act." Well, who does that? People act, then the thinking comes later. Things such as written below:

- "I didn't mean for that to happen like that or go that far."
- "I just wanted to hurt them for what they did to me."
- "I didn't want anybody to get hurt."
- "It wasn't supposed to go like that, I'm sorry."

Now, they want pity or empathy, and they want your forgiveness. Why? Now, you are asking why didn't they think there may be ramifications. Why would they do this? How could they think of doing something so evil? You already know the answer, and it's simple: they didn't think! They acted on their feelings.

Many of us have been in that very same position, with our minds raging out of control when someone says or does something to us to hurt or inflict pain on us. The only difference is some people act on those impulses, and some people know how to control those impulses. They think beyond what's raging through their mind and don't like what could possibly be the outcome if they follow through on those thoughts racing through their mind.

One thing is for sure, you know the devil is real, and it doesn't matter who he uses to hurt you as long as he leaves a path of death, hell, or destruction behind. It doesn't matter who he uses; it can be your mother, father, sister, brother, best friend, or someone you don't even know that will attack you.

His ultimate goal is to strip you to your core and leave you defenseless with a feeling of no hope. It definitely doesn't matter what strategy he uses because his ulterior motive is to annihilate you. Once he thinks you have been defeated by his tactics, he moves on to the next person.

It's kind of like The devil uses the last five of the Ten Commandments against us righteously for all the things we should not do, these are done without hesitation on a daily basis:

6. Thou shalt not kill.
7. Thou shalt not commit adultery.
8. Thou shalt not steal.
9. Thou shall not bear false witness.
10. Thou shall not covet.

Coveting gets many people into all kinds of trouble. Many people have an intense desire to have and take what belongs to another person. There are people that get up and go to work faithfully and work very hard to acquire a few nice things.

Then there are others sitting around working just as hard on a plan to take what someone else has worked hard to gain. They desire to have it as if it rightfully belongs to them so they become fixated on getting whatever the working man has acquired. They would rather have the thrill of taking what belongs to another person rather than try to get up and do something for themselves.

The devil may defeat us in some of these areas of our lives, but Jesus said he came so that we might have life.

There is hope and strength in the name of the Lord. Instead of creating a negative space that will consume you, create a positive space or atmosphere around you to be one you can live with for the remainder of your life.

God has spoken many words of wisdom in my ear as a quiet whisper:

I. The devil is already defeated. If you don't believe it, then he's not defeated.
II. We have victory in him—Christ. If you don't believe you have victory, you don't have it.

This book is dedicated to all the parents that have cried (or are currently crying) from the depths of their soul behind the loss of a child (or children) due to a senseless act of violence.

About the Author

Dinah M. Sullivan has overcome many adversities. Through them all, she's learned to fight her battles in prayer. She likes to encourage and uplift others. She believes there is a greater good and you can retrain your brain. Replace a negative thought with a positive thought. Replace a bad deed with a better deed.

Love and kindness is her motivation. Because of all the hurt she's endured along the way and knowing how it made her feel, she does not want to inflict that same hurt on others. She believes we are all fallible human beings with our own idiosyncrasies. These make us distinct in our own way, so we should have compassion for one another and let love reign supreme.